HARRIET TUBMAN
A JOURNEY TO FREEDOM

Neil Armstrong

Jackie Robinson

Harriet Tubman

Jane Goodall

≫TRAIL BLAZERS

HARRIET TUBMAN
A JOURNEY TO FREEDOM

SANDRA A. AGARD

RANDOM HOUSE NEW YORK

Library of Congress Cataloging-in-Publication Data
Name: Agard, Sandra A., author.
Title: Trailblazers: Harriet Tubman: a journey to freedom / by Sandra A. Agard.
Description: First edition. | New York: Random House Children's Books, [2019] | Series: Trailblazers |
Includes index. | Audience: Ages 8–12.
Identifiers: LCCN 2019010784 (print) | LCCN 2019011234 (ebook) | ISBN 978-0-593-12407-9
(trade pbk.) | ISBN 978-0-593-12408-6 (lib. bdg.) | ISBN 978-0-593-12409-3 (ebook)
Subjects: LCSH: Tubman, Harriet, 1822–1913—Juvenile literature. | Slaves—United States—
Biography—Juvenile literature. | African American women—Biography—Juvenile literature. | African
Americans—Biography—Juvenile literature. | Abolitionists—United States—Biography—Juvenile
literature. | Underground Railroad—Juvenile literature.
Classification: LCC E444.T82 (ebook) | LCC E444.T82 A64 2019 (print) |
DDC 326/.8092 [B]—dc23

Created by Stripes Publishing Limited, an imprint of the Little Tiger Group

Printed in the United States of America
10 9 8 7 6 5 4 3 2 1

First Edition

Contents

ROAD TO FREEDOM

On one moonless night in 1849, a runaway slave ran swiftly toward the Choptank River. Up above, the North Star shone brightly in the sky, guiding her on. She moved quickly and carefully through the trees, keeping close to the shadows. The runaway was on constant alert, wary of any sudden  movements or sounds. She occasionally touched a nearby tree trunk, her fingers brushing the moss to check her direction—her father had taught her that moss mainly grew on the north side of the trees.

Owls hooted, bats flicked back and forth, crickets clicked their wings, and fireflies zigzagged across the path, as if this were any other night in the Maryland woodland. But it wasn't any other night. This was the night Harriet Tubman escaped from slavery for good!

Though she didn't know it yet, this would be the first of many dangerous trips to freedom.

I should fight for my liberty as long as my strength lasted.

⋛ A TERRIBLE TRADE ⋛

Harriet was not the first enslaved person to run away, nor would she be the last. Europeans had been kidnapping, buying, and selling African people since the fourteenth century. The first documented arrival of captive Africans in North America was in 1619. Two English ships captured a Portuguese slave ship in the West Indies, seizing about fifty men and women aboard. The captives were brought to Jamestown, Virginia, where some were sold to settlers. For many years, owners treated these captives as indentured servants.

Slave or Servant?

An indentured servant was someone bound by a contract, known as an indenture, to work for an employer for a certain amount of time, usually between four to seven years. The servant agreed to provide labor in exchange for clothing, food, a place to sleep, and a small wage. When

the indenture came to an end, the servant was freed. Some people chose to enter into these harsh contracts, as it was the only way they could afford passage to the American colonies. Others were forced into indentured servitude—kidnapped and coerced into signing years of their life away.

But indentured labor was expensive—employers had to pay wages. Once freed, former servants could set up their own farms, which meant the plantation owners made less money. Slavery, on the other hand, provided a cheap labor force—as no wages were paid—and less competition. Sugar was brought to the American colonies in the early seventeenth century and, along with cotton and tobacco, proved to be a popular product in America and Europe. Wealthy colonizers established more and more plantations in both the West Indies and the southern states of America to grow these crops. By 1641, Africans arriving in the colonies were no longer treated as indentured servants but as slaves.

Tobacco

Cotton

Sugar

With land up for grabs in newly colonized America but not many people available to work on it, the demand for slavery grew. For almost two hundred years, slave traders kidnapped people from African countries and transported them across the ocean to work on the plantations. This crossing was called the Middle Passage. The difficult journey took up to twelve weeks, with the captives kept in tightly packed, unclean conditions.

The enslaved population grew, and the plantation system became an established way of life. But in 1808, a law came into effect that would change slavery in the South forever. The law made it illegal to bring new slaves into the country—the days of kidnapping Africans and transporting them to the colonies were over. Enslaved mothers became an important source of profit for their owners. The birth of a child not only meant another pair of hands for the harvest; a child born into slavery could be sold, like cotton and sugar, for profit.

LIFE AS AN ENSLAVED PERSON

Men, women, and children were forced to work from sunrise to sunset for no wages. Their owners told them to forget their languages, traditions, stories, and religions.

As an enslaved person you could:

- work up to fifteen hours a day
- be sold or loaned out to another owner at the whim of your master or mistress
- have your children (who automatically became enslaved at birth) taken away from you at any time
- have your home searched every two weeks for weapons or stolen goods

As an enslaved person you could not:

- choose to change your owner, even if you were in danger of being harmed by your current owner
- leave the plantation without permission
- strike your master or your master's children, even in self-defense
- own property
- wear fine clothes

≡ NORTH VS. SOUTH ≡

At the beginning of the nineteenth century, the Northern and Southern states of America had very different beliefs and values.

In the South, farming was big business. Growing crops was much easier when you had a huge free workforce! Slave owners believed that slavery was morally right and often used biblical passages to justify keeping people as property. Although two-thirds of Southerners owned no enslaved people at all, slavery was tied to the region's economy and culture. In fact, by the mid-nineteenth century, there were almost as many black people—both enslaved and free—in the South as there were white people (four million blacks to five and a half million whites).

The plantations stretched from the Chesapeake Bay colonies of Maryland and Virginia south to Georgia. Cotton made a lot of money, and millions of acres were converted to its production. Enslaved people were also crucial to the sugar plantations in Louisiana and the growing of wheat and tobacco in other states.

The North, on the other hand, didn't have the warm climate needed for crops like cotton and tobacco. Instead, the North's wealth was built on industry.

Factories making food, firearms, textiles, and metal products brought in lots of money and attracted people from all over the world to move to America for a chance at a better life. In fact, seven out of eight immigrants settled in the North rather than the South during that time period. The economy of the North had been less dependent on slave labor, and by 1804 all Northern states had voted to abolish slavery within their borders.

The North also built better transportation links, with more than two-thirds of the railroad tracks in the country running across the Northern states. These rail lines made it easier to get from factory to factory, city to city, and helped industrialization to flourish.

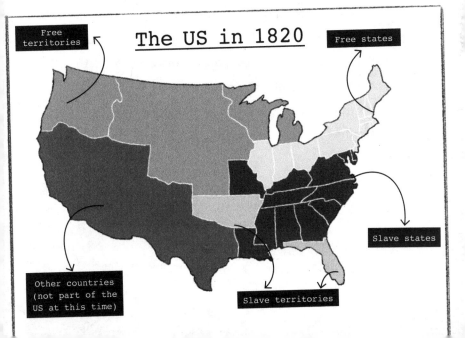

The US in 1820

Free territories

Free states

Slave states

Other countries (not part of the US at this time)

Slave territories

⋚ A SECRET RAILROAD ⋚

This was the cruel world Harriet was born into. Her ancestors came from West Africa, traveling to America on slave ships across the Atlantic Ocean. Though the South had tough laws against helping runaways, there were still people willing to risk their lives to help others be free. In time, Harriet became involved in the struggle for freedom herself.

The Underground Railroad was not a real railroad but an escape network of secret safe houses, known as "stations," along a route to freedom for runaway enslaved people. It was formed around the late 1700s and ran from the South to the free states in the North and Canada. Free blacks, sympathetic whites, and enslaved people themselves aided runaways in their bid for freedom.

Harriet Tubman played a key role in the Underground Railroad, acting as one of the "conductors"—a person who helped runaways on their journey. She led over seventy people out of slavery through a series of clever schemes and ploys. She returned to the South an estimated nineteen times to free other slaves and was known as "the Moses of her people."

But Harriet knew nothing of this as she fled through the woods on that moonless night in 1849. As she walked quickly toward the Choptank River, all she understood was that her journey would be long, difficult, and dangerous. But at the end of it, freedom waited.

She traveled almost one hundred miles on foot, by boat, and by wagon, from safe house to safe house, moving only by night. She had to avoid the patrollers and slave hunters trailing her—as well as their hounds. But when she looked up at the sky and saw the North Star, Harriet found hope.

CHAPTER 1

LIFE IN THE QUARTER

Around 1820, Harriet Tubman was born as Araminta Ross on a plantation belonging to Anthony Thompson, in an area called Peter's Neck in Dorchester County, Maryland. By the time she was two, Araminta and her family had moved to a different plantation, owned by Edward Brodess, near Blackwater River. Though  in time the world would come to know her by the name Harriet, she was called Minty throughout her childhood. There was no actual record of her birth—slave births were not recorded. Her parents, Harriet Greene and Benjamin Ross, could not read or write. They measured important dates by the seasons, not the months. That year would always be known as "the year Minty was born."

Harriet's Hazy History

Harriet never learned to read or write, and few enslaved people had their photos taken, so we don't have any firsthand accounts of what her childhood was like. Lots of what we do know comes from snippets in newspaper articles and books of the time. Later in her life, Harriet worked with an author named Sarah Bradford. Harriet shared her memories with Sarah, who wove Harriet's words into two biographies, which are extremely important for helping us understand Harriet's story.

Bradford did occasionally exaggerate, however, probably in order to make Harriet's story as exciting as possible! Sarah states that Harriet rescued over three hundred enslaved people, but Harriet herself put the estimate much lower.

Old Rit and Ben, as Harriet's parents were known, had several children before Harriet came into their lives. Some of the children lived with them, while others were "hired out" by Edward Brodess to farmers who could not afford to own slaves. Even though slaves were unpaid, owners still had to provide their food and housing—plus it was expensive to buy slaves in the first place. Harriet's brothers and sisters were named Mariah Ritty, Soph, Linah, Ben Jr., Robert, Rachel, Henry, and Moses.

Harriet's family lived in the slave quarters, an area of the plantation made up of long, windowless log cabins with dirt floors and basic fireplaces, built to house from ten to twelve people. The hearth was a continuation of the dirt floor. Often when the wind blew, smoke would engulf the small dwelling, so the cabins had a permanent smoky smell. Harriet's cradle was carved from a gum tree, probably by her father, who was a skilled woodsman.

Harriet's Family

Harriet's parents belonged to different owners. Old Rit was born at Bucktown Farm and was the "property" of Atthow Pattison. On his death, she was passed down to his granddaughter Mary Brodess. In 1803, Mary's husband died, leaving Mary in charge of the farm and their toddler son, Edward. Mary married again, this time to a man named Anthony Thompson, the owner of Madison Plantation, and the owner of Ben Ross. The two properties merged temporarily, and Rit and Ben married. Mary Brodess died in 1809 and left everything to eight-year-old Edward. When Edward was twenty-one years old, he got married and took over Bucktown, taking along the enslaved people he had inherited, including Rit and her children. Harriet was separated from her father, who stayed on the Madison Plantation.

The Brodess plantation was small compared with others in the area. Enslaved people were important to the Brodess family, as their income relied on a good harvest. By 1825, Edward Brodess's farm wasn't making enough money, and he was forced to start selling slaves.

Fear filled the quarters when the "Georgia traders" rode in, the nickname given to any slave buyers who appeared on the plantation. They were eager to purchase strong men and women to take down South to work on the plantations and in the chain gangs—where groups of enslaved people were chained together and forced to work on state building projects, such as constructing roads.

Owners tore families apart with no thought to their feelings, selling men, women, and children to traders heading to different states. Most plantation owners were eager to make some quick money, and Edward was no exception.

TO BE SOLD & LET
BY PUBLIC AUCTION
On MONDAY the 18th of MAY, 1829

For Sale

SLAVES

To be let
MALE AND FEMALE
SLAVES

Also for sale, at Eleven o'Clock
Fine Rice, Gram, Paddy, Books, Muslins, Needles, Pins, Ribbons, etc

When the traders arrived on Brodess's plantation, some of the first ones to go were Harriet's older sisters, Mariah Ritty and then Linah and Soph, sold to an auctioneer named John Mitchell. Harriet stood beside her mother, watching as the slave traders carried off her weeping sisters. It was a sight she would never forget.

The next time Edward's men came for one of Old Rit's sons, Rit refused to open the door of the cabin. Helped by the others in the quarter, she hid her son for a month in the woods. The Georgia traders would not get one of her children this time!

Songs and Spirituals

As the enslaved people were not allowed to read or write, the traditions of music, prayers, laments, dance, quilting, folktales, storytelling, and medicine mixing proved essential for passing on customs.

When the enslaved people were brought to the American plantations, they were forced to forget their African languages and traditions and made to practice Christianity. Still, lots of African cultural and creative customs were handed down through the generations. Songs and rhythms brought from Africa became known as spirituals. Spirituals were often sung as call-and-response songs—where one person would sing a line, and others would repeat it or sing a response. As well as having a strong religious message, spirituals were used by enslaved people to pass the time while they worked in the fields, and to celebrate and remember family histories and folktales. They were also used to convey coded messages of upcoming escapes and resistance (see pages 86–87).

Old Rit told Harriet stories from the Bible about Moses and the children of Israel. Harriet loved to hear these tales of enslaved people escaping from a life of pain and captivity. Her mother also taught her songs like "Go Down, Moses."

Oh, go down Moses

♪ ♪

Way down in Egypt land.
Tell old pharaoh
Let my people go....

♪ ♪

Harriet never forgot these words—they were her
first taste of freedom. Along with her mother's songs
and Bible stories, Harriet heard tales of Africa from
an elderly woman who cared for the small enslaved
children while their parents worked. Though she was
strict and kept a tight rein on Harriet and her friends,
her stories transported the children to a world very
different from their own. The stories spoke of a time
when African people were not enslaved but were able
to determine their own destinies.

"Once, our people could fly," the older woman
would say, beginning one of Harriet's favorite stories.
"But we lost our wings when we crossed the sea and
forgot about our secret power. One day our powers
returned...."

The People Could Fly

The slaves had been in the fields since sunrise. A slave named Sarah was working with her sleeping baby tied to her back. The baby started to cry, but Sarah couldn't stop to feed her.

"Keep that child quiet!" the overseer shouted at her from up on his horse.

The driver, who worked with the overseer, rushed over to Sarah, whip in his hand, ready to beat her and the child. Sarah was so tired and hungry, she could do nothing but fall to the ground.

Toby, another slave, went over and whispered something to Sarah—magic words in an African language the enslaved people had almost forgotten.

Suddenly Sarah and the baby began to float up into the air! The driver tried to stop them, but they floated higher and higher, out of his reach.

The overseer could not believe his eyes. Toby whispered the magic words to other people in the field. Slowly, each slave rose up into the sky and flew away from the plantation. Toby was the last one to fly away.

The woman always ended her story by reminding her young listeners that, sadly, not everyone could fly, and so they must find another route to freedom, even if that meant waiting until the days of slavery were over. Harriet loved that story and believed that one day she would find a way to be free.

⋛ REVOLTS AND REBELLIONS ⋚

As Harriet grew up, hushed whispers told of the growing number of slave revolts around the country, led by men like Denmark Vesey, who had attempted a rebellion when Harriet was a toddler.

Denmark Vesey was a former slave from South Carolina. After winning $1,500 in the city lottery at age thirty-three, he was able to buy his freedom. Denmark had been a sailor and could read and write. He was a member of the African Church in Charleston, an independent church that had been founded in 1817. Denmark's church wanted slavery eliminated, or abolished.

Denmark Vesey was always reading and quoting from the Bible. Like Harriet's mother, he loved the story of the children of Israel. He preached to enslaved people, telling them that all men were created equal and that it was wrong for a man of color to bow and be humble before a white man.

Denmark Vesey became so frustrated with the plight of the enslaved people that he started planning an uprising, intending to kill all the whites in Charleston. The uprising was set for July 1822.

A few days before , Denmark gave one last sermon
to his followers, preaching from the Book of Zechariah
in the Old Testament:

Two of Denmark's loyal followers, Peter Poyas and Mingo Harth, helped make pikes, a kind of long spear. They kept lists of fellow supporters and places where ammunition was hidden. The plan was to assemble in groups around the town, attacking different locations and preventing the whites from banding together. One of the groups, made up of free blacks who owned or worked with horses, would be on horseback.

However, two days before the uprising, the plans were discovered! Civilian militia arrested 131 slaves in and around Charleston. Denmark was identified as the ringleader. After a trial, Denmark and thirty-four of his followers were hanged. None of them had confessed, and Peter Poyas had urged everyone to "stay silent," even as those arrested were being tortured.

There was a sense of disbelief from the white community. Denmark's judges just didn't understand why a free man, with wealth and learning, would consider taking up arms. They told him:

"You had much to risk and little to gain."

This episode frightened the plantation owners. They didn't want their "property" getting ideas about freedom. They issued new laws restricting the movement of the enslaved people even further:

RULES FOR SLAVES

SLAVES CAUGHT ON THE ROAD WITHOUT A PASS WILL BE WHIPPED BY ANY WHITE MAN WHO DISCOVERS THEM.

TWO SLAVES CAUGHT TALKING WILL BE WHIPPED, AS THEY COULD BE PLOTTING A REVOLT.

SLAVES CANNOT HOLD CHURCH MEETINGS.

Old Rit disapproved of all this talk of freedom. She just wanted to care for her family and keep them safe without anyone being sold to the traders. Edward Brodess liked Harriet's parents—he'd promised Old Rit that he would free her and

Edward Brodess

her relatives on his deathbed if they stayed loyal, faithful, and hardworking. Old Rit, who was all of these things, took her master at his word.

Owners saw the enslaved children on the plantation as valuable property and an investment for the future. Children started working in the fields when they were very young, and could be sold away from their mothers at a moment's notice.

Only the very littlest children had any time to play. They played games like "Hide the Switch," where a child hid a piece of tree branch that the other children had to find. The child who found the switch chased the others, attempting to hit them. They also role-played scenes from funerals, slave auctions, family gatherings, and baptisms. Clapping games and dodgeball were favorites, too. But all too soon, playtime was over.

CHAPTER 2

THE WORK BEGINS

Harriet started to work at about four years old. She ran errands between the big house and the fields or acted as a scarecrow, protecting the crops.

By the time she was six, Harriet was expected to be a useful part of the workforce on the plantation. In the searing heat, she carried water to the field hands and picked up leftover pieces of cotton or tobacco.

Roles on the Plantation

Field slaves—men, women, and even children as young as four who tended to the crops in the fields growing cotton, tobacco, and sugarcane. Fieldwork was long and hard. Slaves were expected to toil in all kinds of weather with little food, water, or rest.

House slaves—men and women who worked and sometimes lived in the house of the owner. They had a variety of duties, including cooking, serving meals, cleaning, looking after their owners' children, sewing, doing carpentry, and gardening.

Overseer—a white man employed by owners like Edward Brodess to manage the running of the plantation. The overseer usually sat on his horse watching the field hands, giving orders, and making sure everybody was working hard and quickly.

Driver—usually a trusted field slave who accompanied the overseer. If an enslaved person was not working fast enough, the driver whipped that slave. Drivers were usually disliked by other enslaved people.

A few months after Harriet started working, Edward Brodess had a visit from one of his neighbors, Mrs. Cook, a weaver who was looking to hire out one of Edward's slaves. She wanted to hire a young girl, as she could not pay much. "One of the little girls who are constantly running around the quarter would do," she said. Harriet was called to the big house to meet her. Mrs. Cook was unimpressed. She thought Harriet was too small, but as no one else was offered, she had no choice.

"I will take her," said Mrs. Cook. Before Harriet knew what was happening, she was being driven away in Mrs. Cook's wagon, not even allowed to say goodbye to her family!

⊰ TRAPPED AND TRAPPING ⊱

Harriet was confused and afraid as the wagon took
her farther and farther from everything she had ever
known. Her fear deepened when she saw the new
place where she would live. It looked nothing like the
big house at the Brodess plantation. Instead it was
built from logs and resembled the cabins of the slave
quarters, though it was larger, with two floors.

Harriet was amazed to discover that people slept in
different rooms, rather than sharing one large space
as she had with her family. Harriet, however, had to
sleep in the kitchen in a corner by the fireplace.

She was soon put to work. Mrs. Cook tried to
teach her to weave, but the loom was large, noisy,
and very frightening to Harriet, who had never
seen anything like it before. Mrs. Cook stood over
the loom, constantly moving it back and forth at
great speed. Harriet was expected to stand beside
her, winding the yarn for hours. This proved to be
difficult—not only was she unused to the work, but
she found the noise and the fuzz impossible to deal
with. Harriet sneezed and coughed and kept dropping
the yarn, which was bulky and hard to grip.

Mrs. Cook quickly became frustrated with Harriet, calling her clumsy and careless. "I have no use for the girl," she told her husband. "Maybe you can find something for her to do." Mr. Cook agreed to take Harriet off his wife's hands. He was a muskrat catcher and thought that Harriet could help him check the traps.

Although the water was freezing where the traps were kept, she preferred being outside in the open air. She watched the muskrats closely as they dived from the riverbanks, and she soon learned their habits.

⋝ ILLNESS ATTACKS ⋜

One morning, Harriet woke up with a terrible cold and found it difficult to get up. She received no sympathy from Mrs. Cook, who did not believe Harriet was really ill. Neither did her husband, who sent Harriet out into the water to check the traps. Her eyes streamed as she entered the freezing water. After Harriet returned to the house, she shivered and shook violently on her sleeping mat in the corner of the kitchen. Even Mrs. Cook had to admit that something was wrong with Harriet.

News reached Old Rit that her daughter was ill. She went to Edward Brodess and asked if Harriet could be returned to her care. Edward agreed. It turned out Harriet had caught measles—worse still, she had developed bronchitis by standing in the freezing water. As soon as Old Rit got Harriet back, she made her daughter a hot and bitter drink out of roots from the forest.

It took six weeks for Harriet to get better, but slowly her strength returned, though from that time onward, her voice would always be a bit husky. It was said that later in life when she sang, her rich and deep tone would leave her audience transfixed.

When Harriet recovered, she began playing with the other children again. This happy time was soon to end, though. When Edward heard she was feeling better, he sent her back to Mrs. Cook. To make sure she didn't get ill again, the Cooks insisted that she learn to weave, rather than spend time outside. But Harriet was stubborn—she didn't want to weave or stand in that noisy, lint-filled room. She refused to learn. This angered Mrs. Cook, who thought Harriet was lazy and incredibly stupid.

Harriet's stubbornness continued, and she was returned to the Brodess plantation with Mrs. Cook's insults ringing in her ears. Harriet had won her first victory! There would be more to come.

TROUBLE AT MISS SUSAN'S

During a hot August in 1827, the field hands had to move quickly to harvest the tobacco before the crop rotted and spoiled. That would have made Edward Brodess angry! Tobacco made him a lot of money— and he was always short of money. Many people said he overspent, as he regularly entertained guests who traveled from far and wide and sometimes stayed for several months.

The enslaved people were always anxious at harvesttime because there was the risk that anyone could be sold or hired out away from their families.

Sure enough, Harriet found herself being hired out again later that summer—this time to a woman named Miss Susan, who wanted a nursemaid for her baby son. On arriving at her new home, Harriet was shown her sleeping mat in the kitchen by the stove, then ordered to clean the parlor.

Harriet had never been inside a room like that before and didn't really know what to do. She swept and dusted all the furniture as she'd been told. Harriet gave it her best shot, but her efforts weren't good enough for Miss Susan, who ordered Harriet to clean the room again. Even after a second attempt, Miss Susan was still unhappy.

Miss Susan became convinced that a slave could not be taught anything and would only answer to the sound of the whip. She began to beat Harriet, but Harriet's screams soon brought Miss Susan's sister, Miss Emily, to the parlor. Emily told off her sister for not showing Harriet exactly what to do and said she would leave the house immediately if Susan did not stop the beating. In a rage, Miss Susan left the parlor.

Emily asked Harriet to show her exactly how she had cleaned the room. Once again, Harriet moved all the furniture to the center of the room and swept. Just as she was about to start dusting, Emily stopped her—Harriet needed to wait for the dust to settle before carrying on. Finally, Harriet understood how Miss Susan wanted things to be done—the kindness of Miss Emily had saved her from future beatings.

In addition to housework, Harriet had to look after Miss Susan's baby, who cried all the time because it was unwell. Harriet had to comfort the child and stop it from crying, as the noise upset Miss Susan. If Harriet fell asleep, the child would begin to wail again, and Miss Susan, who kept the whip close at hand, would beat an exhausted Harriet mercilessly.

Harriet was whipped so often that the back of her neck was covered with scars that she would carry into adulthood. Harriet learned to sleep very lightly, aware of the slightest movement or sound around her. Occasionally, Miss Susan and her husband went out to parties. During these times, Harriet let the baby cry loudly while she slept, though she was always listening for the return of Miss Susan's carriage.

Harriet thought of running back to the Brodess plantation, but she did not know which direction to go.

All too familiar with Miss Susan's whip, Harriet started wearing more clothes. The cloth acted as padding against the blows.

⊰ A FIRST ESCAPE ⊱

A few months in, Harriet was waiting to take the baby, when her mistress began to argue with her husband and turned her back on Harriet. There was a bowl of sugar lumps on the table, and Harriet had always wondered what sugar tasted like. She gave in to temptation and took a lump of sugar—but Miss Susan turned around and saw her. Knowing that her punishment would have

been even harsher than usual, Harriet fled, running from the house in a random direction!

She ran past house after house but could not stop at any of them. Everyone in the area knew Miss Susan and her husband and would simply have returned Harriet to their home in disgrace. Finally, Harriet came across a large pigpen. She climbed inside and stayed there for days, fighting the sow and her piglets for food.

Battered and starved, Harriet knew she had no choice but to return to Miss Susan and take her punishment. Sure enough, when Harriet got back to their home, Miss Susan brutally beat her. Then Harriet was returned to the Brodess plantation.

CHAPTER 3

A SHATTERING BLOW

Back at the Brodess plantation, Old Rit had to nurse Harriet back to health—she was nothing but skin and bones, covered with scars both old and new.

When Harriet was well enough, she began to work in the fields. She found this suited her better. She disliked being stuck indoors, her happiness determined by the whims of her white mistresses.

Edward began to hire her out again, and this time she was kept outside. She loaded sacks of flour onto wagons, split wood, tended to and worked with mules, and became an expert in caring for tools such as axes, hoes, and plows.

⋛ RUMORS OF REBELS ⋛

In 1831, Harriet heard about Tice Davids, a runaway slave who had seemed to vanish into thin air after escaping his owner. Stories began to circulate that he must have gone on the "underground road." Rumors of a secret railroad were rife—Harriet, like so many others, believed that there was an underground train that would take escapees from the South to the North.

When Harriet was about eleven, there was a second uprising, this time led by a man named Nat Turner. Nat was enslaved and lived in Southampton County, Virginia. He had learned to read and write and had become fascinated by stories from the Bible. He saw visions, which he said came from God. He became a preacher and was called "the Prophet" by his followers.

On August 20, 1831, Nat Turner held a meeting on the plantation where he lived. He gave a risky and passionate speech to his followers, urging them to fight for justice and their freedom. "I am to slay all the whites we encounter, men, women, and children," he told them. The crowd were inspired—was it finally time for them to rise up?

Nat and his followers set off at nightfall. At every plantation they passed, more people joined them. The rebellion had started. Along the way, they killed around sixty white people—men, women, and children—on various plantations.

Local militia finally stopped the uprising. The authorities cracked down hard, and an estimated one hundred enslaved people were killed. But Nat Turner could not be found. He stayed hidden in a cave in Southampton County for two months, until eventually a farmer discovered his hiding place. Nat Turner was tried, convicted, and then executed on November 11, 1831, in Jerusalem, Virginia. But the story did not end with his death—his actions were being talked about everywhere.

Harriet and the other enslaved people on the Brodess plantation heard the stories of the uprising. Thoughts of freedom once again entered her mind.

Owners were very worried. Not only were talkative slaves thought of as suspicious, but those considered too quiet were also deemed dangerous and were sold. Further laws were passed that enforced even stricter rules on the enslaved people. Singing "Go Down, Moses" was banned. But the plantation owners could not stop the stories of the revolts from circulating.

51

The Dangers of Reading

To limit communication among enslaved people, state governments put several laws in place that made it illegal for slaves to read or write. Between 1829 and 1834, Alabama, Georgia, Louisiana, North Carolina, South Carolina, and Virginia passed strict anti-literacy laws. In South Carolina, anyone teaching enslaved people to read or write would be fined 100 pounds and face six months in prison.

Harriet was so good at working outdoors that she was often called to perform back-breaking tasks like lifting heavy goods, mending fences around the plantation, and digging and turning the soil. She developed the work-hardened palms of a field hand.

Edward was pleased with her progress; this small and sullen girl was finally making him some good money! He hired her out at every opportunity, and in 1834 she went to work on a harvest for a man named Barrett.

End of the Harvest

The end of the harvest was usually a joyful time for everyone on the plantation, from the big house to the slaves' quarters. Plantation owners would hold parties for friends and neighbors—there was much cause for celebration. Enslaved people held contests such as "Shuck the Corn." This involved the corn being heaped into two piles. Teams competed to see who could remove the husks the quickest and shrink their pile first. As they worked, singers would lead call-and-response songs.

Harriet was in the field, joining the others in the chorus as she watched the corn mounds get smaller. She noticed one of the field hands standing silently by the pile of corn, not singing but edging ever so slowly away from everyone. Harriet saw that the overseer was watching him, too. Since the Nat Turner rebellion, all plantations had been on the alert for slaves who were too quiet or sullen. Plantation owners feared they might be thinking of escape or rebellion. Suddenly the field hand began to run toward Bucktown!

The overseer ran after him. Harriet gave chase to see what would happen. Down at the crossroads, the field hand rushed inside a small store, closely followed by the overseer, who ordered him to stop, threatening him with a beating.

"Hey, you! Stop that boy!" he yelled at Harriet, spotting her as she came into the store. The runaway bolted out through another door. Harriet's next decision would affect the rest of her life: she moved toward the door, blocking the overseer.

He was furious and picked up a lead weight, throwing it after the runaway. It missed him but hit Harriet on the head. She fell to the ground unconscious.

Punishments for Running Away

Enslaved people could:

- have a foot, or half a foot, cut off to stop them from running again
- be set upon by their master's dogs
- be whipped and/or shackled in front of all the other slaves
- be sold to another plantation owner, away from their family
- be branded with the letter "R" for "Runaway"

To slave owners, any punishment was acceptable for a runaway slave.

The cut to Harriet's head was deep. She was carried back to the slave quarters by some nearby field hands. Once again, Old Rit had to treat her daughter's terrible injuries. As she watched her young daughter lying so still on the straw mat, she might have been thinking of her daughters Mariah Ritty, Linah, and Soph—sold down South—and praying that she would not lose another child.

Many people from the quarter came to visit Harriet as she lay in a deep sleep, including Edward Brodess. Nobody thought she would survive. The wound was severe, and she was in a coma for two days. When she finally woke up, Harriet was seriously ill and too weak to stand. Even though she was so sick, Edward tried to sell this troublesome young slave. Much to the relief of her family, nobody wanted her.

Harriet's recovery was long and difficult. She stayed in the cabin from harvest until March, to the annoyance of Edward Brodess, who was making no money from her. As Harriet made the slow journey to recovery, she prayed that Edward would change his ways and become a kind Christian man.

Harriet's Sleep Disorder

As a result of her injury, Harriet suffered from narcolepsy—a brain disorder that caused her to fall asleep at any moment—along with painful headaches.

NARCOLEPSY

1 in 2,000 people have narcolepsy.

It is caused by the loss of brain cells that produce a chemical called hypocretin.

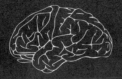

SYMPTOMS

- excessive daytime sleepiness
- disrupted nighttime sleep
- sleep paralysis and hallucinations
- intense dreaming or nightmares
- sudden episodes of muscle weakness

Harriet also began to have strange dreams every night. She believed that they were visions sent from God. She dreamed of horsemen riding in to kidnap the enslaved. She heard the hooves of horses and the screams of the women as their children were ripped away from them.

Harriet prayed passionately to be freed from slavery. She dismissed the teachings of the New Testament that called for slaves to be obedient and faithful. Instead, she discovered that the teachings of the Old Testament, with the stories of deliverance from oppression, were more inspiring to her.

Then the Lord said to Moses, "Go to Pharaoh and say to him, 'This is what the Lord, the God of the Hebrews, says: "Let my people go, so that they may worship me."'"
—Exodus 9:1

The other enslaved people on the Brodess estate began to look to Harriet for guidance. The fact that she had survived three near-death experiences (the measles at the Cooks', the whippings at Miss Susan's, and the iron-weight incident) and now seemed to be having holy visions led them to think she had been touched by the hand of God.

Edward Brodess didn't have such admiration—as soon as Harriet was feeling better, he hired her out to a builder named John Stewart. To Harriet's delight, this meant moving back toward the Madison Plantation and working alongside her father, Ben.

Ben was charged with leading the workforce who cut and hauled timber. He was an expert in the treatment of woods and was even allowed to travel from the timber yard in Madison to towns and cities along the Chesapeake Bay, an estuary leading into the Atlantic Ocean. At the bay, big logs were loaded onto boats and sent to the shipbuilders in Baltimore. Rather than join her father in the timber yard, Harriet was set to work in John Stewart's house. But being cooped up cleaning still didn't suit Harriet at all.

She asked John Stewart if she could work outside in the woods with the men. Stewart had seen her carry enormous logs to the fireplace and haul huge cauldrons of hot water from the cookhouse to the stream at the back of the house—he knew her strength matched that of the men working in the woods. He also knew that he would be getting a good bargain, as it was cheaper to hire women than men. He agreed, but he warned

Harriet that if it did not work out, she would be sent back inside the house to do chores.

John Stewart need not have worried. Harriet was now in her comfort zone, in the open air and beside her beloved father, and she excelled at her work.

Between 1820 and 1832, enslaved and free black people had dug a seven-mile canal through the Stewart family's marshy land. Once it was built, mariners like Harriet's father floated logs and other produce along it to Madison Bay. Out of the hearing of their masters, these men discussed freedom in the North and the dangerous obstacles along the way.

John was very happy with the results and decided that Harriet could "hire her time." That meant Harriet could find work for herself and pay Stewart fifty or sixty dollars a year from the income she made—whatever she earned over and beyond this sum, she kept with his permission. This practice was a privilege, and only the most trustworthy, hardworking enslaved people were allowed to do it.

Stewart even took to parading Harriet in front of visitors, showing off her strength and skills. She was as strong as any man on any plantation, and he wanted everyone to see this small woman—Harriet was just five feet tall—complete these amazing feats. Stewart would order Harriet to drag a boat loaded with stones along the riverbank as if she were an ox or mule.

CHAPTER 4

A BIG DECISION

Over the six years that Harriet worked at Stewart's timber yard, Harriet eagerly looked for outside work. One day she would be cutting down trees and hauling logs, the next she would be plowing the fields or driving an oxcart and tending to mules. She became a familiar figure in the fields—a short, slender young woman with her skirt tucked into a rope around her waist and a colorful bandanna tied on her head.

Her father educated her about the natural world, teaching her the names of the birds and demonstrating their calls. Ben taught her which berries were safe to eat and which were poisonous. He showed her the plants that had cured her when she'd caught measles and bronchitis. Harriet's father also taught her:

- how the water lily, the leaf of a cranesbill plant, and the back of hemlock could be used as medicine if she got sick or injured.

- what sounds birds make when disturbed

- that moss usually grows on the north side of trees

- how the rivers and streams ebb and flow

- how to tell the direction
  of the wind by licking
  a finger and sticking
  it up into the air

- how to work out
  north and south
  from the direction of
  flocks of birds

- how to read the sky and
  spot the North Star—the
  only star that remains
  constant

One of the most important lessons Ben taught Harriet was how to choose a path through the woods without making a sound. All his efforts were rewarded when one day she followed him through the trees and crept up on him, making him jump out of his skin!

They never spoke about why he was teaching her these skills, but in later life, Harriet reflected that her father was probably preparing her for the day that she would leave. Neither of them knew that Harriet would need to put these new skills to the test all too soon.

In 1840, not long after Harriet had started working alongside her father, Anthony Thompson passed away, leaving his estate to his son, Doc Thompson. He left behind a will promising that Ben Ross would become a free man on his forty-fifth birthday. Harriet's father was no longer a slave.

⋝ FIRST LOVE ⋜

When Harriet was a young woman, she met and fell in love with John Tubman, a free black man from Dorchester County. John's parents had been given their freedom at the time of their owner's death, and so he had been born free. Marriage between a slave and a free black person was not uncommon in this part of the country. It was an informal arrangement rather than a legally bound union, and the marriages were unstable, because the enslaved person was always at risk of being sold. Any children resulting from the union would follow their mother's status. If their mother was free, the child would be free. But if Harriet and John had children, they would be born enslaved and automatically become the property of Harriet's owners—the Brodess family.

Despite these restrictions, in 1844, John asked Edward Brodess if he could marry Harriet. The answer was yes. They were soon "jumping the broom," a ceremony where enslaved people could seal their commitment to each other in marriage. The bride and groom would jump over a broom handle held a few inches off the ground. It signified the couple's entrance into their new life together— and the creation of a new family—by sweeping away their single lives.

Harriet made a brightly colored, nature-inspired patchwork quilt as a sign of her love for John. Around this time, she discarded her childhood name, Minty, and took her mother's name, Harriet, instead.

⋛ DREAMS OF FREEDOM ⋚

For a few years, Harriet and John lived together
in harmony at the Brodess plantation. But in
December of 1848, news came to the quarter that
Edward Brodess was going to sell Harriet along
with her brothers, Ben Jr. and Henry. Harriet was
terrified—she knew she would never survive the
journey, as she still fell asleep at random moments
and had horrible headaches. Once she had one of
her spells, she would be left at the side of the road;
she had no doubt about that. Traders wanted money
quickly, and they would not care for a sick slave!

Harriet changed her prayers to God. Now, instead
of praying to convert Edward, she prayed for his
death. Coincidentally, a few days later, Edward
became sick. Not long after, he died. It's unknown
what actually caused Edward's ill health, but Harriet
was devastated, as she felt her prayers had caused
his death. There was new panic among the enslaved
people—what would happen to them now? Would
anyone be sold? Edward had promised many of the
enslaved people, including Old Rit, their freedom. How
could this promise be honored, now that he was dead?

Harriet decided to pay a lawyer five dollars to look at the will of Old Rit's first owner, Atthow Pattison. It took a long time for Harriet to save the money, but it was worthwhile when she learned the truth. Harriet's mother had been mentioned in Atthow's will, which stated that on Atthow's death, Old Rit was to have her freedom at the age of forty-five.

But Pattison's granddaughter Mary and her son, Edward, had chosen to ignore the will. Harriet's discovery was disheartening, and her unhappiness grew. She wanted to be free like her husband and like her father. She wanted her family to be free, too.

Since the incident with the iron weight when she was a child, Harriet was still having narcoleptic spells where she could fall asleep at any moment. She had several episodes a day. It was always unsettling, as she never got any warning of when she was going to have an attack. Harriet's strange, vivid dreams persisted, too. She repeatedly dreamed that she was flying over fields of cotton and corn, over the settlement of Cambridge and the Choptank River to the mountains. But then she always reached a barrier. It would take different forms—sometimes it was a fence, other times a mountain, but the outcome was always the same— she could never cross it. Then the dream would take a more positive turn. . . .

It appeared like I wouldn't have the strength, and just as I was sinking down, there would be ladies all dressed in white over there, and they would put out their arms and pull me across.

Harriet received no sympathy from her husband, John, when she told him about her dreams. He felt it demonstrated how restless she was becoming. "How can a person have the same dream over and over again," he'd say. He would laugh at her and tell her that these fanciful dreams kept coming back because she was losing her mind. But as Harriet's dreams continued, John became angry. Especially when Harriet began to talk about the North Star. She told him that when she saw it in the night sky, it was as if it were calling to her and telling her to follow it.

"John, we can go together. We will both be free," she would say. But John did not agree. He told her running away was wrong and that they had a good life. Besides, how would they survive in the dark and dangerous woods? What direction would they go? What would happen if they got lost? What would they eat? But Harriet persisted, telling him she could survive in the woods by using the information her father had taught her.

John refused to agree to Harriet's plan. He was quite satisfied with living on the plantation. They had been married for nearly five years, and although they still had no children, they had been happy.

Harriet was shocked by her husband's threats to tell the master if she tried to run away. John was starting to seem like a complete stranger to her. She knew then and there that she would no longer tell him about her dreams or the rising voice inside her that cried for freedom. Any plans for escape she had, she would now have to keep to herself. She could never trust him again!

⹀ HARD TIMES ⹀

In 1837, cotton had brought thirteen cents a pound—which meant that a strong field hand could sell for as much as a thousand dollars. However, by 1845, cotton was selling at only five cents a pound, and the field hands were going for less than five hundred dollars. Over the next few years, prices continued to fall. Plantation owners were taking great losses. When Edward Brodess died, he had left all his debts, too. His wife, Eliza Brodess, would have to sell some of his slaves to pay off the money he owed.

In 1849, Harriet was working in the field near the edge of the road when a white woman driving a wagon approached her. The woman was a Quaker. She had been watching Harriet and was curious to know how she had come to have such a deep scar on her forehead. Harriet told the story of the flying iron weight, which had missed its actual target but hit her

with such force that she was unconscious for days. The woman was sympathetic, and from that day on she stopped to chat with Harriet every time she saw her. The woman told her that if Harriet ever needed help, she could visit her farm near Bucktown. Harriet thanked the woman and went back to work; she didn't want to draw the attention of the driver or overseer.

Quakers

The Quakers were a religious group founded in England in about 1648. Many Quakers emigrated to the English colonies in America, partly because they wished to convert others to their faith.

They led peaceful and simple lives, had few possessions, and wore plain clothes. Many Quakers opposed slavery because they believed in equality for all. By the 1780s, the leaders of the movement had barred their members from owning slaves. They became one of the first organizations to take a stand against both slavery and the slave trade.

The Pennsylvania Abolition Society, a group largely made up of Quakers, took part in protests and wrote essays detailing the wrongs of slavery and the slave trade. Many safe houses on the Underground Railroad belonged to Quakers.

Edward Brodess had stated in his will that none of his slaves should be sold outside of Maryland, but everyone knew that because of the lack of money, his wife would ignore this restriction. If slaves were sold farther afield, families would be ripped apart and lives ruined forever. Conditions in the Deep South were harsher than those in Maryland. On the large, sprawling plantations, slaves were expected to toil in the hot sun all day, watched over by brutal overseers. The deeper south you were sold, the less likely your chances of ever escaping or seeing your family again.

Harriet now had thoughts of running away daily, and the North Star was calling to her. She didn't want to attempt the journey by herself, because she could fall asleep at any time. As traveling with her husband was now out of the question, Harriet asked Ben and Henry to run away with her.

After some persuasion, her brothers agreed to go, and the three of them made plans to meet near the edge of the forest. Harriet made them promise not to tell anyone—not even their parents.

On the chosen night in 1849, Harriet made sure John was asleep before she slipped out of the cabin. Her brothers were waiting for her at the agreed spot, and they began their long and dangerous journey.

Almost immediately, everything went wrong. Her brothers were not as familiar with the woods as Harriet, and even though she led the way, they kept tripping on roots or crunching leaves beneath their feet. Harriet was horrified by the amount of noise they made. Henry and Ben Jr. complained that it

was too dark to see where they were going, and they startled at every sound.

Henry and Ben decided to turn back. Running away was too dangerous, and despite their sister's pleas, they wouldn't take another step. They didn't want their foreheads branded with the letter R for runaway, and they certainly didn't want to have a foot cut off. To Ben and Henry, freedom wasn't worth the risk. But Harriet wasn't ready to give up and told them she would go on alone. Unimpressed, her brothers told her she had to turn back, too. Bigger and stronger than the five-foot Harriet, they forced her to return to the plantation with them.

It's not clear how long they were gone, as there are different versions of this story. Some accounts say it was only a night, whereas others suggest it was over a week! Whatever the truth, they got away with it. Back at the plantation, Harriet slipped into her cabin next to her sleeping husband. She was bruised and scratched but not disheartened. If anything, her first taste of freedom just made her more determined that next time, it would be different. Next time, she would go alone.

CHAPTER 5

ON THE RUN

A few days later, as Harriet toiled in the fields, a fellow field hand signaled to get her attention. She worked her way toward the man, who was digging at the soil. He quietly told her that a trader was arriving at dusk. She was going to be sold.

For a moment, Harriet's mind went blank. Her time had come at last. She had no choice but to run alone, and to run that night. She might fall asleep or suffer one of her horrible headaches, but it was a risk she was prepared to take.

"There was one of two things I had a right to: liberty or death. If I could not have one, I would have the other; for no man should take me alive."
—Harriet Tubman

At dusk, she and the others stopped working and made their way back to the slave quarters. Harriet desperately wanted to let her mother know that she had made the decision to run away, but as a field hand, she could not go into the big house, where her mother worked. She considered taking the risk and began walking the path that led to the house when Doc Thompson drew up in his carriage, returning from business in Bucktown. He had been taking care of the running of the plantation since Edward's death. Her plan to say goodbye to her mother was foiled—but Harriet couldn't bear to leave without her mother knowing.

Struck by inspiration, Harriet began to sing. Her deep, loud voice seemed to grow wings and fly toward the big house.

Her voice was poignant and soothing, and all those who heard it were moved. Even Doc Thompson stopped to listen. He loved to hear the enslaved people sing, because it showed they were happy. He never knew that messages were being passed along in the songs.

When that old chariot comes,
I'm going to leave you,
I'm bound for the promised land,
Friends, I'm going to leave you.
I'm sorry, friends, to leave you,
Farewell! Oh, farewell!
I'll meet you in the morning,
When I reach the promised land.

Songs as Codes

Singing was very important to enslaved people for a number of reasons, not least because the lyrics could help to convey secret messages. Certain songs were known as map songs—the hidden meanings gave people directions. "Follow the Drinking Gourd" was one example. On the surface, "drinking gourd" just meant the water dipper that enslaved people used to collect water, but its coded meaning was the Big Dipper—the formation of stars that point northward, the direction a runaway should head. Some other hidden messages in songs used on the Underground Railroad include:

Wade in the water...

Meaning: Get in the water!

Meaning: It's safe to approach!

Meaning: Stay hidden; there's danger nearby.

Meaning: I'm planning to escape!

⋛ HARRIET'S ESCAPE ⋜

That night, Harriet went about her usual chores. John was hardly speaking to her these days, and they spent most evenings in silence. When she knew John was sound asleep, she got up quietly and helped herself to some ash cake (a type of bread), a piece of salt herring, and her wedding quilt.

Rather than set off into the woods, Harriet decided to head for Bucktown to the farm on the edge of the town. She was going to ask that white woman she had met by the road for assistance. It was a risky move—although the woman had said she'd help, Harriet couldn't know whether she'd really meant it, or how committed she would be to her offer once she discovered that Harriet was a runaway.

She uttered a quick prayer, walked toward the woman's door, and gently tapped on it. In the stillness of the night, the knock sounded so loud. The door opened, and the Quaker woman appeared. To Harriet's great relief, the woman nodded and asked Harriet to come in. She led Harriet into the kitchen and told her to sit down. She wrote two names on a piece of paper, then gave Harriet directions of where to go next.

The first stop, or station, on the Underground
Railroad was another farm; Harriet couldn't miss it—
there were two white posts with round knobs on them.
The people there would give her food and clothing and
keep her safe until it was time to move to the next place.

Harriet was overwhelmed by the kindness of this woman and wanted to repay her generosity. The only item of any worth Harriet had with her was the patchwork quilt. She gave the beautiful blanket to the woman in gratitude.

Harriet left the house, walking through the woods until, early the next morning, she came across the farm with the two white posts.

When she knocked on the door, a woman opened it, took the note from Harriet, and offered her some food. Once Harriet had eaten, the woman gave her a broom and told her to sweep the yard. For a second, Harriet hesitated—she hadn't left the plantation to be forced to work for someone else! Then she realized that pretending to be the woman's maid would be a good cover-up if anyone came by looking for a runaway slave. She took the broom and began to sweep.

As night fell, the woman's husband brought a wagon to the side of the farm. He told Harriet to climb in and then filled the wagon with produce. He covered her with some blankets and set off along the bumpy track. When the wagon finally stopped, they were by the Choptank River. He told her to follow the river to the next safe house, but to travel only at night, because by now the slave hunters would be trying to trail her. She must stay off the road at all cost!

⋛ A LONG JOURNEY ⋜

The details of the rest of Harriet's journey are hazy. Her exact route is unknown, due to the secrecy that surrounded the freedom roads. The route she probably took was northeast along the Choptank River and through Delaware to Pennsylvania. In total, she traveled about ninety miles, but there's no record of how long that trek took.

   Harriet's journeys along the Underground Railroad included many "stops"—stores, homes, and businesses of abolitionists and sympathizers—where runaway slaves could find hospitality. Though she never recounted the names of those who helped her, in later years she recalled some pretty memorable experiences along the way, including:

- a free black family concealing her in a potato hole in their cabin

- a man rowing
  her up a river
  in silence

- a Quaker
  woman hiding
  Harriet in
  her attic

Harriet herself wasn't really sure of what route she took—knowing only that she fixed her eye on the North Star, trusting it to lead her to freedom.

She did remember how she felt when she crossed the Mason-Dixon Line—the boundary between Maryland and Pennsylvania that marked the northern limit of the slave-owning states. Beyond the Mason-Dixon Line lay freedom. When Harriet finally crossed into the free state of Pennsylvania, the sun was rising.

I looked at my hands to see if I was the same person now I was free. There was such glory over everything. The sun came up like gold through the trees and I felt like I was in heaven.

By this time, a notice had appeared in the newspaper offering a reward of three hundred dollars for Harriet's capture—using her childhood name, Minty. It was signed by Eliza Brodess.

THREE HUNDRED DOLLARS REWARD

Runaway from the subscriber on Monday 17th: MINTY aged about 27 years, is of a chestnut color, fine looking, and about 5 feet high.

Eliza Ann Brodess

⋛ FREE AT LAST ⋚

Harriet was unaware that there was a price on her head. She traveled on to Philadelphia. This city contained the largest community of people of color in North America, with over 20,000 black men, women, and children living in the area. For those who wanted to journey north, it was the first stop on the road to freedom.

Between June 1849 and June 1850, a total of 279 enslaved people fled Maryland, just like Harriet. It was the highest number of fugitives to leave a slave state in one year. Many of them wound up in Philadelphia—a hub of culture and industry that offered a fresh start.

Harriet had mixed feelings about the city. Although she was free, she was also alone. She was surprised by the fine clothes and educated manner of speaking that people of color had here, and she discovered that many of them were runaway slaves, too.

Harriet was very homesick and found the busy, noisy streets of Philadelphia overwhelming. She longed for the woods and her family, wishing they could also be free. She wanted to rescue them, too. But how could she go back without getting caught?

I was a stranger in a strange land.

Harriet found work as a cook in a hotel. She had never liked domestic work, but she knew she needed money if she was ever going to return to Maryland and save her family. For a year, she prepared food, washed dishes, and scrubbed floors. She saved up her meager wages and tips.

In early 1850, she visited the office of the Philadelphia Vigilance Committee, an organization that dealt with all the enslaved fugitives who came to the city, helping them to cope with their new lives. At any hour of the day, the committee would offer food, clothing, money, a place to hide, or even a job reference. It was at their office upstairs in Lebanon Seminary that she met William Still, the secretary of the Vigilance Committee.

William Still

William Still was a free black man, his
mother having escaped from her owner
when he was just a little boy. In 1844,
at the age of 23, William migrated
to Philadelphia, where he joined the
abolitionist circles. He played a central
role in the abolitionist movement, risking
jail for sheltering fugitives. He also
kept a record of the people who passed
through his station on the Underground
Railroad, making careful notes that were
hidden in a cemetery until after the Civil
War, and would later be used to help
reunite families.

Harriet began visiting the office regularly. From William and others, Harriet learned about how the Underground Railroad worked and the secrecy involved. She became familiar with some of the conductors of the railroad. They included:

- Dr. James Bias, a black doctor who gave shelter to runaways

- Robert Purvis, a mixed-race abolitionist who hid runaways in a room behind a trapdoor in his house and served as president of the Pennsylvania Anti-Slavery Society

- William Whipper, a white sympathizer, whose house was continually crowded with runaways. After a night's rest hidden in Whipper's house, runaways would be transported in his boxcar to Philadelphia or Pittsburgh. William Whipper was never jailed for his actions, but his lumberyard was burned on many occasions for suspected anti-slavery activities.

Harriet heard how the runaways sent coded messages back to their families to let them know that they were safe in their new homes. There were a few ways of doing this. She could have:

- dictated a letter that would have been sent to a free black person living near her mother's plantation, telling that person that she was safe. It was vital that the information was included cryptically, as Southern postmasters often examined mail that was delivered to black people.

- passed a message along the grapevine of the Underground Railroad. Just as runaways traveled north along it, messages could be passed back down South

- made a secret arrangement with a sympathetic white person to smuggle a letter back to her family.

One way or another, Harriet got word to her mother and father that she was safe and well within a year of her escape.

The more Harriet heard of the Underground Railroad, the more determined she became to help the organization by sharing her own experiences of her journey to freedom.

CHAPTER 6

THE UNDERGROUND RAILROAD

During one Vigilance Committee meeting, Harriet heard the news that a free man named John Bowley wanted help getting his wife and two children from Baltimore to Philadelphia. Unless he got them off the planation, they were going to be sold down South. John Bowley's wife, Kizzy, was Harriet's niece. Harriet immediately said she would guide them to safety, but William Still was reluctant to involve her. Harriet was a fugitive, and it was difficult enough for free black people to move in the South, let alone those being hunted by the law. Plus, Baltimore was an extremely dangerous place for runaways. Any black people traveling by boat or train were required to present free papers for inspection.

But Harriet was determined to rescue her niece and her children. She had already seen her sisters sold—she was not going to let that happen to her niece. She helped to devise a plan and got ready to make the grueling journey back down South.

HARRIET'S FIRST RESCUE

Kizzy's chance to run away did not come until December 1850, when she and her two children were literally on the auction block in Cambridge, Maryland, waiting to be sold.

As instructed by the Vigilance Committee, her husband, John Bowley, took advantage of the auctioneer's dinner break and delivered a note to the auction house, pretending it had come from the auctioneer himself. The note said the auctioneer had found a buyer elsewhere, and John was to take Kizzy and the children away. His family members were handed over to him.

Kizzy, John, and the children hurried down the street to a safe house. They stayed in the attic until it was dark. In the evening, after a rushed meal, the safe house owner took them to a farmer's wagon, told them to lie down, and covered them with blankets. The carriage trundled along to the river, where John was surprised to see a white woman standing beside a small fishing boat.

Who are you? she asked.

A friend with friends! John replied.

It was the password he had been told to say. The woman stepped away from the boat and told John and his wife to climb in with their children. She covered them with sacks of potatoes and onions, wrapping the baby under a shawl she had been wearing over her coat. They set off, rowing across the bay to Bodkin's Point on the Chesapeake's western shore, and arrived at a stable, where they ate some food before resuming their journey. This time, they only traveled a short distance to a house.

Inside, Harriet was waiting for the family, dressed as a man. She had made it to Baltimore from Philadelphia by moving from station to station. While she'd waited for her niece, Harriet had taken the opportunity to explore the city. She became familiar with the nooks and crannies, back roads and alleyways, and got to know the conductors living in the area.

When Kizzy entered the warm kitchen, she stopped short at the sight of Harriet before rushing forward to embrace her aunt. Harriet's disguise had not fooled her niece!

They stayed in the house in Baltimore for a week before leaving to carry on their journey north. Harriet had brought along a pistol, paid for by her earnings from the hotel. With this gun for protection, and a growing knowledge of the land between Baltimore and Philadelphia, Harriet led the party from safe house to safe house, on foot, by boat, and by wagon. Within a year of her own escape, she had become a conductor of the Underground Railroad. Under her guidance, John Bowley and his family all made it to safety. Harriet's first rescue was a success!

⋛ THE "BLOODHOUND LAW" ⋚

When she reached Philadelphia, Harriet took Kizzy, John, and the children to the Vigilance Committee. There, they heard about a terrifying new act that the government had passed while they were away. It was called the Fugitive Slave Law. This new law stated that anyone convicted of helping or hiding fugitives would be imprisoned for up to six months and fined $1,000. This law included not only the South but the North as well. It was nicknamed the "Bloodhound Law," because slave catchers were using dogs to track down missing runaways!

Escaped enslaved people could be shot, whipped, and sold again. Runaways were afraid that neighbors would give them up to the authorities. Some ex-slaves, even those who had lived in Philadelphia freely for decades, felt too unsafe to stay and moved even farther north, toward Canada.

HARRIET'S CONDUCTING CONTINUES

The new law did not stop Harriet. She felt confident she could help more enslaved people reach freedom, just as she had helped her niece's family. In the spring of 1851, Harriet undertook her second rescue mission. She once again made the risky journey back to the Brodess Plantation and tried to persuade her husband, John Tubman, to return with her to the North. But he had settled down with a new wife, Caroline. He refused to go with Harriet—in fact, he even refused to see her! Harriet was heartbroken, as part of her had really believed that they could make a life together in the North.

After this blow, Harriet's priority was to leave as quickly as possible. As long as she remained near the plantation, she was in danger of being recognized. Despite her husband's choice, her rescue mission wasn't a wasted journey. She gathered a small group of enslaved people willing to run away, including one of her brothers.

Codes on the Road

Users of the Underground Railroad often adopted code words to communicate messages or instructions with each other. Lots of these code words took inspiration from the railway or from the Bible.

CODEWORD:	MEANING:
bundles of wood	runaways that were expected
Canaan	Canada
cargo	runaway enslaved people who needed transporting on the Underground Railroad
conductor	person who directly transported enslaved people
forwarding	taking enslaved people from station to station
freedom train	Underground Railroad
French leave	sudden departure
shepherds	people who encouraged enslaved people to escape and helped them
station or stop	safe house or other place of safety
stationmaster	keeper or owner of a safe house

After leading her brother and the others to safety, Harriet was determined to gather more funds so she could plan further rescues. Once again, she returned to working as a cook and a maid. She moved from place to place over the summer and finally settled in Cape May, New Jersey. The Fugitive Slave Law had made life uncomfortable for people like Harriet, as slave catchers could now legally capture and return fugitives to their owners.

Being a slave catcher could be a profitable profession, as owners were willing to pay a lot of money for their "property" to be brought back. People put up posters warning former slaves to be on the lookout when the catchers were in town.

FUGITIVE SLAVES

ATTENTION

The slavehunter is among us!

BE ON YOUR GUARD!

AN ARREST IS PLANNED FOR TONIGHT

BE READY TO RECEIVE THEM

WHENEVER THEY COME

FREEDOM FOR HER FAMILY

In the winter of 1854, Harriet set out to free more members of her family. Around Christmastime, she planned to rescue her brothers Henry, Ben Jr., and Robert from the Maryland plantation.

She dictated a coded letter to a literate friend, who posted it to Jacob Jackson, a free black man living near her father. She trusted Jacob would get word to her brothers. Harriet used biblical phrases to convey her message—even though she couldn't read, she knew the Bible very well. She said:

> Read my letter to the old folks, and give my love to them, and tell my brothers to be always watching unto prayer, and when the good old ship of Zion comes along, to be ready to step aboard.

The letter was signed "William Henry Jackson." The authorities intercepted the letter and read it to Jacob. He said it was a case of mistaken identity—he did not have a family member named William. The authorities suspected there was more to it, but had no way of proving it.

Luckily, although the letter was taken away, Jacob had understood Harriet's code and conveyed the message to her brothers. They prepared to leave the plantation as Harriet made the journey down South. Once she got there, though, there was a delay. Ben Jr.'s fiancée was expecting a baby. Ben wanted to watch the birth of his child and make sure his fiancée and new baby were well before leaving.

While they waited, Harriet went to visit her father, whom she had not seen for several years. Knowing that in the future he would be questioned about the disappearance of his sons, he blindfolded himself before Harriet came in. Later, when his sons were discovered missing and he was asked if he had he seen his daughter, he could therefore honestly say no. In fact, he had not "seen" his sons, either! Harriet was overjoyed to be with her father again, and he was proud of her for all she'd accomplished.

Harriet sadly never saw her mother. It was decided that due to Old Rit's "excitable nature," it was better that Harriet did not visit her.

Once the baby had been born, Harriet took her brothers all the way to Canada. They crossed the border in December 1854. On this journey, it is likely that she used Frederick Douglass's safe house in Rochester, New York. Frederick was a social reformer and a leader of the abolitionist movement as well as a gifted orator. His speeches and anti-slavery writings proved just how wrong slave holders were in believing that enslaved people lacked the intelligence to be independent citizens. Frederick Douglass persuaded many Americans to become abolitionists. In his autobiography, he wrote:

"On one occasion, I had eleven fugitives at the same time under my roof, and it was necessary for them to remain with me until I could collect sufficient money to get them to Canada."

Although he does not mention Harriet Tubman by name, the size of the group and the timing suggest that he was describing her party. There was understandably so much secrecy involved in the Underground Railroad network that it's difficult to determine exactly what happened and who was involved, even today!

Around this time, abolitionist newspaper *The Liberator* nicknamed Harriet "Moses." Just like the biblical Moses, Harriet took her people to freedom. The nickname caught on, and her legend was truly born. All over the country, her exploits were talked about in the enslaved cabins, the plantation houses, and parlor rooms.

After Harriet's early rescues, her life fell into a rhythm. She rented a house in St. Catherine's, Canada, through the winter, chopping wood to earn money. In the summer, she headed to New Jersey or Pennsylvania and worked in hotels. She made at least one trip a year to the South, setting out alone but always returning with "cargo."

Her travels took her far and wide. She would move runaways through Wilmington, Philadelphia, and New York City as she traveled from the Mason-Dixon

Line to the Canadian border. Wherever she went, she made reliable contacts. She would take back roads and always travel at night, and usually in the fall, as the shorter days meant more hours to travel. Now and then, Harriet would be hit by a spell of narcolepsy, and her passengers would be forced to wait patiently for their guide to wake up and continue the journey!

In order to keep all of her passengers safe, Harriet sometimes had to treat the enslaved people quite harshly. From her first-ever escape attempt with her brothers, she knew that fear could ruin everything. Although she carried a pistol on each journey for protection, she never had to use it—but she'd occasionally threaten to kill anyone who lost their nerve. She even once drugged a baby who wouldn't stop crying! This was a common practice at the time.

Despite these tough measures, Harriet's reputation as a successful conductor grew and grew, because she never lost a passenger. While she was gaining legendary status among the Underground Railroad, she was fast becoming a thorn in the sides of slaveholders and slave catchers. The authorities of the South were determined to catch this woman who avoided and outwitted them at every turn.

≥ CHOOSING HER CARGO ≤

Harriet never set foot on a plantation during her
rescue missions in the South. She spread the word
that she was in the area by singing:

"Go Down, Moses."

The message that she was nearby would be passed
from one slave to another. Sometimes she sent out
false information to root out possible betrayals.
Once she was sure that nobody was going to give
away those planning on escaping, she would send out
a final message.

Saturday night was the usual time for departure,
as owners normally treated Sunday as a day of
rest. Many enslaved people went to visit family and
friends on a Sunday, too, so anyone who left with
Harriet on a Saturday night would not be discovered
until Monday morning. Then the owner could not get
any Wanted posters printed until Tuesday. The slave
catchers and their bloodhounds that frequented the
suspected routes of the Underground Railroad were
a risk, but often by the time they were deployed, the
trail would have gone cold.

⋛ FAME AND FORTUNE ⋚

As she grew more famous, it became difficult for Harriet to make as many trips down South as before. Still desperate to help the Underground Railroad's efforts, in 1858 she began lecturing at locations all over the North. Her firsthand accounts of the Underground Railroad and its workings proved very popular, and she raised even more money to help fugitives, station masters, and conductors fighting to free slaves.

She was invited to speak in the parlor rooms of high society in Concord and Boston. In these anti-slavery speeches, Harriet told fascinating stories of her narrow escapes. Money poured in as more and more people heard about her amazing rescues.

⋛ HARRIET'S STORIES ⋚

One time, Harriet was traveling during the day in her home state of Maryland. She was wearing a large sunbonnet and kept her head bowed, but when she passed a former employer, Harriet worried that she would be recognized. Luckily, she'd just bought a couple of chickens at the market.

Thinking quickly, she opened the cage of chickens, which fluttered and squawked, causing an awful noise and diverting attention from herself.

On a different occasion, Harriet was traveling in a railroad car and noticed two gentlemen quietly discussing whether she was the woman on the Wanted poster at the station. Never one to panic, she simply picked up a newspaper and began to "read" it. Harriet Tubman was known to be illiterate—so this woman reading the paper studiously surely could not be the fugitive!

END OF AN ERA

One of the last successful trips Harriet made was to rescue her parents in 1857. They were now both too old to work and had been given a cabin, a horse, and a cow. It was a conscious, if difficult, decision for Harriet to leave these two most beloved people until last. If Harriet had taken her parents away before her brothers and the others, there was a good chance these young and strong slaves would have been sold farther down South.

By the time Harriet went to collect them, her father was due to be tried the following week for having helped a slave escape. Harriet later remarked that she had helped out the state, as she had "saved them the expense of the trial" by stealing her parents away.

Old Rit and Ben were too elderly to make the long trip by foot. The ever-resourceful Harriet Tubman put together a makeshift wagon and coaxed a horse from a field, transporting her parents all the way to Canada.

In the spring of 1859, Harriet bought a house in Auburn, New York, from the senator and abolitionist William Seward, for the reasonable price of $1,200. Her mother and father, having struggled through the cold Canadian winters, moved in with their daughter.

A Rising Tension

After several conflict-ridden trials where runaway slaves had been returned to the South following the introduction of the Fugitive Slave Law, more and more Northerners were speaking up against slavery.

At the end of 1860, Abraham Lincoln was elected president. He was anti-slavery, so many Southern states disagreed with his vision for the country and didn't want him as their president. In response to his election, South Carolina became the first state to secede— or leave—the United Statesthe United States. Within a few months, several other states including Georgia, Mississippi, Texas, Florida, Alabama, and Louisiana also left. The country was splitting apart, and tensions were rising.

Harriet's final rescue mission was in November of 1861. She wanted to keep going back to Maryland to rescue more people, as she had become restless with the lecture tour and longed for a more challenging activity. However, her friends in the abolitionist movement were concerned for her safety. They did not want her to return to the South.

Slave owners were furious with the woman who kept helping their "property" to escape. They put up posters, demanding her capture and promising a big payout for anyone who found her. The price on her head put her at huge risk; it put the runaways she aided at risk, too. Harriet would have to give up conducting on the Underground Railroad for good.

WANTED!
Dead or Alive
HARRIET TUBMAN
For helping fugitives escape on the Underground Railroad

In 1861, the war that had been threatening the country finally broke out. The Civil War was fought between the United States of America and the Confederate States of America, a new country made up of eleven Southern states that had seceded from the United States. There is still a lot of debate about the causes of the war, but the South's desire to preserve slavery was certainly a key factor.

NORTH　　**SOUTH**

The president of the Confederate States was Jefferson Davis. However, Abraham Lincoln wanted to reunite the United States—and abolish slavery. The states that remained loyal to the United States were known collectively as the Union; those that seceded were known as the Confederacy.

CHAPTER 7

NURSE, TRACKER, SPY

As a woman and an African American, Harriet's options to join the war effort were limited. But John Andrew, the governor of Massachusetts, asked Harriet for her help. He'd heard her speak at the high-society lectures and believed her knowledge of the Underground Railroad and her experience as an enslaved woman would be invaluable. Even though she couldn't read or write, Harriet was able to remember complex instructions, memorize difficult directions, and think on her feet. Governor Andrew asked Harriet if she would join the state's volunteers who were heading to Port Royal Island off the coast of South Carolina.

Ultimately, he wanted Harriet to become a spy. Harriet agreed. It was dangerous—she was still a wanted woman—but this was a way to help end slavery for good!

While Harriet was preparing for her trip, the fighting continued. A terrible battle at Shiloh, Tennessee, left around 4,000 soldiers dead and over 27,000 wounded. The scale of the battle shocked the nation.

⋛ PORT ROYAL ISLAND ⋚

In 1862, when Harriet arrived at Port Royal Island, South Carolina, the area was in utter chaos. Thousands of Northern soldiers were stationed there, waiting to be called to battle, and they'd been joined by almost as many runaway slaves who wanted to fight, too. Harriet's official role was to assist these newly escaped slaves, but her secret mission was to find out as much information as possible that would help the Union troops.

This proved to be difficult for a number of reasons! Most of the runaways spoke Gullah, a mixture of English and African languages that is unique to the coast of South Carolina and the nearby islands. Harriet found it hard to understand them.

They were also annoyed that Harriet had an army food ration, and they didn't. But Harriet refused to stop trying. She gave up her right to collect rations, and instead sold homemade pies and root beer in the evenings to make money to buy food. Slowly, Harriet got to know the other runaways and they began to trust her.

Harriet supervised the building of a laundry house with her own money and even trained a group of African American women in laundry management. She wanted them to develop skills they'd need in order to hold down jobs once they were free.

⋚ HEALING HANDS ⋚

Port Royal was full of sickness. Soldiers were dying from outbreaks of malaria, typhoid, yellow fever, cholera, and typhus. Harriet became a nurse, helping out in the hospital and caring for the sick.

One of the biggest causes of death was dysentery. This horrible disease spread very quickly through contaminated water, accounting for almost 100,000 deaths across the two armies over the course of the war. Harriet was sure she could help cure the sickness if she could find some of the same roots and herbs that grew in Maryland. One night, she searched the woods until she found water lilies and cranesbill. She boiled the roots and made a bitter-tasting brew, offering it to one of the sick soldiers.

Slowly, the soldier began to recover. The medicine had worked! Harriet gave the drink to other soldiers and made further remedies for illnesses.

Despite spending hours at the bedsides of dying patients, she never became ill. To those who knew the amazing stories about her, this was just another of Harriet's miracles!

⋝ SCOUTING AND SPYING ⋜

For ten months, Harriet tended to the sick. Secretly, she had been building up a network of scouts— escaped slaves who were willing to help her gather intelligence. These trusted scouts worked with Harriet to map the territories and waterways, heading out on missions to survey the land. In 1863, President Lincoln issued the Emancipation Proclamation.

All slaves in Confederate states are now free!

This had little immediate impact because the slave owners in the Southern states no longer answered to Lincoln and ignored this legislation. It did, however, have huge symbolic significance. If the Union and Confederate states were ever to reunite, slavery would be abolished across America. Harriet was overjoyed. Now that Lincoln had done the "right thing" and set the enslaved free, she believed God would let him defeat the South.

The proclamation also meant that Southern black men could now officially join the Union army. They formed their own all-black regiments, though they were still under the command of white officers.

During the war, black regiments made up one-tenth of the Union army. However, about one in every five black soldiers died, a rate 35 percent higher than that of white Union troops killed. Sixteen black soldiers received medals of honor after the war.

One of these regiments' leaders, the white officer Colonel James Montgomery, asked Harriet if she could scout for his troops. Harriet received one hundred dollars from government funds. She went on dangerous missions, slipping behind enemy lines and approaching enslaved people who had accompanied their masters in the Confederate army. She paid them for crucial information, such as the location of other Confederate troops or the position of cannons. Harriet was made commander of Intelligence Operations and had nine scouts under her command.

⟩ COMBAHEE RIVER RAID ⟨

On the evening of June 1, 1863, three Union gunboats left Beaufort, South Carolina, heading for the Combahee River. Shortly after they left, one boat ran aground in St. Helena Sound, but the other two continued on early the next morning. The boats carried about three hundred black soldiers, along with Colonel Montgomery and Harriet. They journeyed along the Combahee River into Confederate country. The plan was to destroy the railroad tracks that ran alongside the water and the bridges that crossed it to cut off the Confederate supply routes. Then, the boats would head farther upriver to burn down several plantations—the homes and fields of influential Southerners. The Confederate army had laid deadly mines along the route, but thanks to the

intelligence Harriet had gathered about the bombs'
positioning, the boats drifted through unharmed.

The party sailed through the night, occasionally
drawing toward the banks to pick up fugitives waiting to
be rescued along the river. The enslaved people working in
the fields had initially been wary of the ships when they'd
seen them approaching, fearing it was a trap, but Harriet

spread the word that the boats would carry them to freedom. More than 750 people came aboard the Union gunboats that night. Harriet later said, "I never saw such a sight. . . . Sometimes the women would come with twins hanging around their necks . . . bags on their shoulders, baskets on their heads, and young ones tagging along, all loaded, pigs squealing and chickens screaming."

The soldiers disembarked and marched south, burning plantations as they went. By the time the Confederate troops had rallied, the Union soldiers were back on the gunboats and out of range. The Confederates only managed to prevent the escape of one slave.

The raid was a total success. The Southern states lost many prized plantations that night and never fully recovered. Harriet became the first and only woman to organize and lead a military operation during the Civil War. Confederate reports would even begrudgingly acknowledge that the Union troops seemed to have an in-depth knowledge of the rivers and countryside.

The first account of the raid, in the Union publication *The Commonwealth*, didn't name Harriet.

CAMPAIGN ON THE COMBAHEE

Col. Montgomery and his gallant band of 300 black soldiers, under the guidance of a black woman, dashed into the enemy's country, struck a bold and effective blow, destroying millions of dollars' worth of commissary stores, cotton, and lordly dwellings. . . .

Days later, another article named Harriet in full on the front page! She was now catapulted into the international spotlight with people all over the world singing her praises. The monarch of Great Britain, Queen Victoria, invited her to England. Harriet was unable to go, but gratefully received the queen's gift of a cream silk-and-lace shawl.

Despite her fame, Harriet still faced hardship. Returning on leave to Auburn from Virginia with her nurse's pass, Harriet bought a half-fare train ticket, as was usual for soldiers and other employees of the government. But the train conductor was having none of it and told her they did not accept black people at half fare. Plus, he said, her papers were forged—no black woman would actually be given those papers! She was asked to leave the seat. Harriet politely refused. With the assistance of three other men, the conductor hauled her out of the carriage and threw her into the baggage cart, likely breaking her arm in the process. Nobody came to help her.

$\gtrless$ END OF THE WAR $\lessgtr$

The war ended in April 1865, when the South surrendered. The Confederacy collapsed, and the 13th Amendment permanently abolished slavery in the United States. However, Southerners weren't going to be converted overnight. They may have lost the war, but many white Southerners still believed that black people were inferior to white people. A difficult road lay ahead.

With the end of the war, Harriet finally arrived in Auburn, New York. Although her service in the Union army was well publicized, she had difficulty getting a pension from the government and came back with little to show for her achievements.

Despite being almost penniless, Harriet always left the door of her home open to anyone in need. Several former enslaved people stayed at her house until they were able to find work. To put food on the table and support their needs, Harriet grew fruit and vegetables in her back garden and kept pigs. She was not ashamed to ask for food donations or borrow money from friends.

In 1868, the 14th Amendment granted African Americans US citizenship, protecting the rights of freed slaves after the Civil War.

A NEW LOVE

After discovering that her husband, John, had died—killed in a street fight with a white man—Harriet found she could finally put their troubled relationship behind her. She fell in love with a Civil War veteran, a man named Nelson Davis, who had once been sheltered in her home.

Nelson was a brickmaker, around twenty-two years younger than Harriet. He had been enslaved near Elizabeth City, North Carolina, but had escaped from his owner and fled to upstate New York. Harriet had met him during the war, and their paths crossed again once the war was over. They got married in March 1869 by the Reverend Henry Fowler at Auburn's Central Presbyterian Church.

PUT IN WRITING

An author named Sarah Bradford asked Harriet if she could write her biography. Harriet agreed—partly because she needed the money, and partly because she hoped her experiences would shed light on the horrors of slavery and the importance of the Underground Railroad. As Harriet told Sarah her life story, the two became close friends.

In 1869, *Scenes in the Life of Harriet Tubman* was published. It opened with a letter of recommendation from Frederick Douglass. He wrote:

The difference between us is very marked. . . . I have wrought in the day—you in the night. I have had the applause of the crowd . . . while the most that you have done has been witnessed by a few trembling, scarred, and foot-sore bondmen and women, whom you have led out of the house of bondage, and whose heartfelt "God bless you" has been your only reward.

The book was a success, and Harriet and Nelson were comfortable for a while. In 1874, they decided to adopt a young girl called Gertie.

Nelson had tuberculosis and had to give up work, so Harriet was left to earn all the income for the household. Although Sarah Bradford's biography helped, there were a lot of mouths to feed, as the house was always full of guests. Harriet repeatedly requested the pension she was due for her war work, but it was refused. Harriet's role had never really been official, so it was difficult to know how to proceed in attaining the money she was due!

In 1888, Nelson died of tuberculosis. As if it could help ease her pain, Harriet was finally granted a pension of eight dollars a month—but only as a widow of a Civil War veteran. Many people took up her cause, and an increased pension was discussed in Congress. Eventually, her pension was raised to twenty dollars a month—eight dollars as Davis's widow and an additional twelve for her service as a nurse.

With these small funds, she established the Harriet Tubman Home for the Aged on a property adjacent to her own, moving many of her house guests into this new property and welcoming others from far and wide. She also paid for brain surgery to try to ease the symptoms from the head injury that had plagued her since childhood.

⋛ VOTES FOR WOMEN ⋜

Throughout the nineteenth century, only men could vote in the United States. Establishing equal rights for women, including voting rights, was a slow process. The first real fight came around the time that slavery ended. The 14th Amendment meant that African American people would be given more rights. While most people felt this was essential and important, some famous women's rights activists, including Elizabeth Cady Stanton, said it would degrade women if black men got the vote before white women. These racist attitudes made people of color feel left out of the conversation.

Frederick Douglass was angry about these comments. Although he was loudly in favor of women's voting rights, he explained the difference between black and white suffragists in a passionate speech:

"When women, because they are women, are hunted down through the cities . . . when they are dragged from their houses and hung upon lampposts . . . when they are in danger of having their homes burnt down over their heads . . ."

Harriet took up the cause of women's suffrage with the same determination she had shown for abolition of slavery. Harriet believed in equality of all people—white or black, man or woman. When asked whether women should have the vote, Harriet replied:

I suffered enough to believe it!

She began touring again in upstate New York, Boston, and Washington D.C., giving speeches about her life. She would describe her years as "Moses," talking about what freedom meant to those who had been enslaved. She said that freedom went beyond ending slavery. Women needed the vote to be truly free.

In 1896, Harriet was invited to speak at the first meeting of the National Association of Colored Women. As always, her speech was dramatic and extremely popular. She was an excellent storyteller, and although Harriet was becoming frail, she gave a spirited address. A few years later, Susan B. Anthony, social reformer and women's rights activist, introduced Harriet at a women's suffrage convention as "a living legend." It was at this gathering that Harriet delivered her famous words:

In 1905, a women's activist named Emily Howland shared a train ride to Rochester with Harriet. They were attending a suffrage meeting the following day. On arriving in Rochester, they said their goodbyes and parted. Emily set off to her hotel, but there was no such luxury for Harriet. She spent the night sitting upright in the train station.

The next day, when Emily realized where Harriet had slept, she was very upset. Emily was ashamed of her own thoughtlessness—she hadn't even asked her friend where she was staying. It hadn't crossed her mind that the area would have no safe and comfortable lodgings for a woman of color. At the convention, Emily not only offered Harriet her room but confronted the organizers. She demanded that they show more compassion by providing lodgings for black women who wanted to attend the meeting.

The campaign for women's suffrage would be a long one. At the end of the 19th century, Wyoming, Idaho, Utah and Colorado gave women the vote, and by 1920, women in all states across the US were able to have their say in the election for the first time.

In 1911, a frail Harriet moved into the home for the elderly she herself had opened. People would come to see her and read her the newspaper. She remained particularly interested in the struggle for women's rights. In her last months, she had a visit from her friend Mary Burnett Talbert. "Tell the women to stand together," Harriet instructed Mary as she left.

In 1913, Harriet died of pneumonia, surrounded by her friends and family. "I go to prepare a place for you," she told them before she passed away.

She was buried with military honors in Auburn's Fort Hill Cemetery. A bronze tablet was placed on the front entrance of the courthouse. It reads:

IN MEMORY OF
HARRIET TUBMAN

WITH IMPLICIT
TRUST IN GOD SHE BRAVED
EVERY DANGER AND
OVERCAME EVERY
OBSTACLE

CONCLUSION

A WOMAN NAMED MOSES

Harriet Tubman will always be remembered as one of the bravest and most daring conductors of the Underground Railroad. But her life affected so many more people than the fugitives she personally accompanied to safety. Her legacy is full of courage, determination, inspiration, and hope. She risked her own life again and again, so that as many people as possible might find freedom, happiness, peace, and safety.

On June 24, 1908, Harriet had told her local newspaper:

"I did not take up this work for my own benefit, but for those of my race who need help. The work is now well started, and I know God will raise up others to take care of the future."

This captures the spirit of Harriet Tubman perfectly. No matter what the odds were, she kept going, because failure was not an option. As William Still wrote in his journal:

Harriet Tubman is not afraid. The idea that she could be caught at any time doesn't seem to enter her head.

Harriet was a superb storyteller with an incredible memory. As she went from gathering to gathering telling her tales, she would be given a cup of tea with butter in it—just the way she liked it.

As she sipped the buttered tea, she told her listeners about the Underground Railroad and that first flight to Canada, the first snows, the sound and smells of the woods, and how it felt to follow the North Star. Riveted by her descriptive words, songs, and prayers, her listeners saw and heard the mighty Niagara Falls as Harriet and her passengers crossed the border to Canada. They felt the joy of freedom as the once enslaved threw off the shackles of their oppressors at the Combahee River Raid. Harriet had the power to make her listeners relive her experiences. She had the power to make her listeners come together.

⋛ A LONG ROAD AHEAD ⋛

Harriet lived to see the enslaved people of America become free. With freedom, African Americans could learn to read and write, giving them greater opportunities for education and different kinds of jobs. It was now legal for them to get married and to own a home. The fear of a family member being sold was gone.

But it would be a long time before black people shared equal status with white people in the United States. Although slavery was over, racism wasn't. The governments across the South introduced laws known as Black Codes, which made it illegal for black people to testify against white people in court or to have weapons.

Many states in the South introduced further strict rules to keep black and white people separate. Together, these restrictions were called Jim Crow laws. Under Jim Crow, in some states, white and black people couldn't get married to each other, eat at the same restaurant, or even use the same bathrooms.

"Separate but equal!" was the cry of the South. But this was far from the truth. Black schools and hospitals were often in poorer condition than the white facilities, and they received very little funding from the government.

In the 1830s, a white actor named Thomas Dartmouth Rice performed routines as the fictional Jim Crow, a caricature of a clumsy, dim-witted slave. As his popularity grew, "Jim Crow" became a widely used, unkind term for black people.

Racist groups sprang up, including the Ku Klux Klan. They made black people's lives miserable and dangerous. They threatened, hurt, and even killed anyone who didn't "follow the rules."

In the 1950s, African Americans had had more than enough of prejudice and violence against them. With the support of many white people, they began a fierce fight for equality that went on for nearly twenty years. From boycotting buses and restaurants to marching on Washington and delivering powerful speeches, people all over the country stood up and said, "Enough is enough!" By 1968, the government had passed several significant laws to put black people on an equal footing with whites. Fifty-five years after Harriet's death, the law finally recognized black and white people as equal.

EDUCATE DON'T SEGREGATE

ENOUGH IS ENOUGH!

WE DEMAND EQUAL RIGHTS NOW!

BOOKS, MOVIES, AND MONUMENTS

In 1886, to help with Harriet's money worries, Sarah Bradford wrote a second biography called *The Moses of Her People*. This volume dived deeper into Harriet's story and sold well across the country.

Since Harriet's death, countless other authors have told her story, piecing together the information we have from her life. In 2019, the feature film *Harriet* was released, telling the story of Harriet's first escape from slavery and her later journeys on the Underground Railroad.

"People know about her achievements, but they don't know of her, the woman. My task is to tell the story of the human being that became the superhero."
—Cynthia Erivo, who plays Harriet

In Maryland, the beautiful, scenic Harriet Tubman Byway winds across 125 miles of countryside, following a similar route to the runaway herself.

The store at Bucktown where the overseer struck Harriet with the weight has been preserved as a museum, and a visitor center on the route contains information and artifacts from the Underground Railroad.

$\gtrless$ PENSIONS PAID $\lessgtr$

Harriet never received her full pension, but in 2003 Senator Hillary Rodham Clinton urged the US Senate to pay the sum of $11,750 to the Harriet Tubman Home, in her memory. In 2016, the US government announced that Harriet would be the new face on the twenty-dollar bill, in honor of her courage, persistence, and service to the country. By 2019, however, this was put on the back burner. It's still unclear whether the twenty-dollar bill will be changed. It currently features President Andrew Jackson, who was a slave owner.

A ROLE MODEL FOR THE FUTURE

While legal slavery is fortunately a thing of the past, there remain many injustices in our society. It's important to celebrate and be inspired by extraordinary people like Harriet Tubman, who remind us to look around at the problems that surround us and take positive action to tackle them. Despite having the odds stacked against her from birth, Harriet showed enormous drive and imagination, constantly looking for ways to improve the lives of those around her. She worked tirelessly and took big risks, with no guarantee of success, in order to do the right thing and make a lasting change to the way people of color were treated and how they were able to live their lives. This woman was one in a million. What do you find most inspiring about her story?

"God's time is always near. He set the North Star in the heavens. He gave me the strength in my limbs. He meant I should be free."
—Harriet Tubman

Timeline

Harriet Tubman is born as Araminta "Minty" Ross.

The first railroad carriage in the US is built in Maryland.

c.1820   1822   1829

Denmark Vesey plans a revolt with the intent to lay siege on Charleston, South Carolina. The plot is discovered. Vesey and thirty-four others are hanged.

The Fugitive Slave Act is passed.

1849   1850   1851

Harriet Tubman runs away, following the Underground Railroad to Philadelphia.

Harriet undertakes her first rescue mission. She helps her niece, her niece's husband, and their two children escape slavery.

Nat Turner leads a short and deadly rebellion in Southampton County, Virginia. Stricter slave laws are put in place after this rebellion.

Frederick Douglass publishes *Narrative of the Life of Frederick Douglass, an American Slave.*

1831 1844 1845

Araminta "Minty" Ross marries John Tubman and changes her name to Harriet Tubman.

Harriet begins lecturing in New York, sharing her stories of the Underground Railroad. She buys a house in Auburn, New York, where she cares for her aging parents.

1857 1859 1860

Harriet helps her parents escape to freedom, leading them to Canada.

Abraham Lincoln is elected president.

President Lincoln
issues the Emancipation
Proclamation. Under
Colonel James Montgomery
of the Union army, Harriet
Tubman leads an armed raid
at Combahee Ferry.

1861

1863

Southern states
secede from the US,
and the Civil War
begins. Harriet
Tubman travels to
Port Royal with
the Union army.

By this year, every
state in the former
Confederacy has established
a set of regulations and
rules to keep black and
white people separate,
known as Jim Crow laws.

1886

1910

Sarah Bradford
publishes a second
biography about
Harriet Tubman:
*The Moses of her
People.*

Harriet marries Nelson Davis, a veteran of the 8th US Colored Infantry.

Sarah Bradford publishes the first biography of Harriet Tubman, *Scenes in the Life of Harriet Tubman.*

1865   1869

The 13th Amendment abolishes slavery throughout the US. Abraham Lincoln is assassinated. The Ku Klux Klan is formed in Tennessee. Mississippi becomes the first state to introduce Black Codes.

1913

Harriet Tubman dies.

Further Reading

→ *Harriet Tubman: The Moses of Her People* by Sarah Bradford (Carol Publishing Group, 1994)

→ *Harriet Tubman: The Road to Freedom* by Catherine Clinton (Little, Brown and Company, 2005)

→ *The Story of Slavery* by Sarah Courtauld (Usborne Publishing, 2007)

→ *What Was the Underground Railroad?* by Yona Zeldis McDonough (Grosset & Dunlap, 2013)

Websites

→ harriet-tubman.org

Information about Harriet Tubman, including facts, quotes, and a photo gallery.

→ harriettubmanbyway.org

The official website of the Harriet Tubman Underground Railroad Byway, including a map and guide to the route, along with information about the freedom trail and its conductors.

Glossary

ammunition: A supply of weapons.

auctioneer: A person who runs auctions by taking bids.

biography: An account (usually a book) of someone's life, written by somebody else.

bloodhound: A large breed of dog with a good sense of smell, used for tracking.

Canaan: An ancient region between the River Jordan and the Mediterranean. In the Bible, Canaan is the promised land of the Israelites.

colonizer: A settler who establishes control over an area.

Confederate States: An unofficial country of eleven pro-slavery states that fought against the Union during the American Civil War.

Glossary

Constitution, US: A document outlining the laws and principles by which the US is governed.

driver (slavery): A supervisor of slaves at work.

dysentery: A disease often passed through contaminated water that causes severe diarrhea and sometimes death.

fugitive: A person who has run away.

Gullah: An English-based language that contains elements from African languages, unique to the coast of South Carolina and the nearby islands.

immigrant: A person who moves from one country to another to live permanently.

indenture: A contract binding one person to work for another for a given time period.

Glossary

industrialize: To develop manufacturing factories on a wide scale.

loom: A frame or machine for making cloth.

Mason-Dixon Line: The boundary from the southwest corner of Delaware north to Pennsylvania—usually considered the boundary between the Northern and Southern states of the United States.

Middle Passage: The voyage of enslaved Africans across the Atlantic Ocean to the Americas.

Moses: A prophet from the Bible who led the Israelites out of slavery.

muskrat: A water-dwelling rodent with shiny brown fur and webbed hind feet.

narcolepsy: A condition where the sufferer has brief attacks of deep sleep, sometimes with hallucinations.

<u>Glossary</u>

overseer (slavery): An employee of a plantation owner who would oversee the day-to-day running of the plantation.

plantation: An estate where crops such as sugar, cotton, coffee, and tobacco are grown.

secede: To withdraw formally from an organization or union.

slave quarters: Buildings designed to house enslaved people on a plantation.

spiritual: A religious song, derived from the mixing of Christian hymns and traditional African music.

suffrage: The right to vote in political elections.

Union states: Twenty-three anti-slavery states that fought against the Confederacy during the Civil War.

veteran: A person who served in the armed forces.

Index

Index

Index

Index

Index

FOLLOW THE TRAIL!
TURN THE PAGE FOR A SNEAK PEEK AT MORE TRAILBLAZERS BIOGRAPHIES!

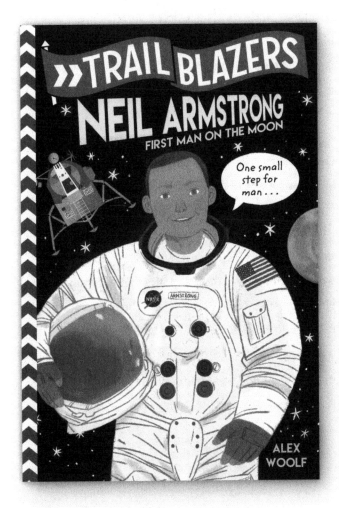

⋛ FLYING LESSONS ⋚

Airplanes remained Neil's first love. His dream was to become both a pilot and an aeronautical engineer— someone who designs and builds planes. About three or four miles outside Wapakoneta was Port Koneta Airport. Neil cycled or hitchhiked there as often as he could to watch the planes land and take off, and talk to the pilots.

When he was fifteen, Neil began saving up for flying lessons. He got a job at Rhine and Brading's Pharmacy, where he earned forty cents an hour. A one-hour flying lesson cost nine dollars, so he had to work twenty-two and a half hours to pay for one lesson! Neil supplemented his earnings at the pharmacy by offering to wash down the airplanes at Port Koneta. He even helped the airport mechanics with some routine maintenance work, servicing the planes' cylinders, pistons, and valves.

Eventually, Neil had saved up enough money to pay for some lessons. A veteran army pilot named Aubrey Knudegard taught him. They flew in a light, high-wing monoplane called an Aeronca Champion.

Aircraft Fact File

Name:	Aeronca Champion
Nickname:	"Champ"
Length:	21.5 ft. (6.6 m)
Wingspan:	35.2 ft. (10.7 m)
Engine:	65 horsepower
Top speed:	100 mph (161 kmh)
First flight:	April 29, 1944

⇒ WALKING ON THE MOON ⇐

Buzz soon followed Neil out, and the two of them explored the lunar surface. "It has a stark beauty all its own," remarked Neil. Buzz described it as "magnificent desolation." The powdery soil was quite slippery, they discovered, but walking was no problem. They unveiled a commemorative plaque that had been mounted on *Eagle*'s base.

They planted a US flag, stiffened with wire to make it look like it was flying in a breeze. Neil photographed Buzz saluting it.

President Richard Nixon called them by radio-telephone from the White House. "This certainly has to be the most historic telephone call ever made," he said. "I just can't tell you how proud we all are of what you've done. . . . For one priceless moment in the whole history of man, all the people of this Earth are truly one."

Neil and Buzz spent the rest of the EVA collecting rock and soil samples and performing experiments. They set up devices to sense moonquakes and to measure the distance between the moon and Earth. Those devices would stay on the moon.

TRAIL BLAZERS
JACKIE ROBINSON
BREAKING BARRIERS IN BASEBALL
UCLA
Life is not a spectator sport.
42
KURTIS SCALETTA

Jackie at UCLA
1939–1941

→ **Football:** Jackie is called "the greatest ball carrier in the nation." In 1939, the Bruins go undefeated, though three games end in ties.

→ **Basketball:** Dazzling play by Jackie helps end a long losing streak by the Bruins but isn't enough to give them a winning season.

→ **Baseball:** Jackie once again plays short and gets a reputation for stealing bases but goes into a hitting slump he can't break out of.

→ **Track and Field:** Jackie sets a conference record and wins the NCAA title for the long jump.

→ **Combined:** Jackie is the first athlete at UCLA to "letter" in four sports—meaning he has significant playing time at the varsity level.

⋛ LOVE AND WAR ⋜

Jackie continued to shine in his second year at ULCA, but the football team and basketball team both had losing seasons. Something happened that was more important than sports or even his education. He met a student named Rachel Isum. Jackie was drawn to Rachel's intelligence and compassion.

At first, he later wrote, Jackie experienced a new kind of prejudice. Rachel Isum knew he was a star athlete and had seen him play. She was convinced he was cocky and full of himself. But as she got to know him, she learned Jackie had a serious mind and—more important—respected that she had one, too. After they'd known each other for a year, they were deeply in love.

No matter what happens, this relationship is going to be one of the most important parts of my life.

Jackie's appeal crossed color lines. Author Myron Uhlberg wrote of how his deaf father connected with Jackie because they were both out of place in the world. Bette Bao Lord wrote a fictionalized memoir called *In the Year of the Boar and Jackie Robinson*, about how Jackie's courage helped her overcome her own barriers as a Chinese immigrant. Anyone who had ever been told they didn't belong, or who stood out for their differences, felt a connection.

And some fans loved Jackie simply because he was an exciting player to watch. He would get on base, take a lead, and dare the pitcher to make a throw. He was always a threat to steal. He would steal third base with two outs. He would steal home! Some fans compared him to baseball's all-time greatest base runner, Ty Cobb. Jackie's fearlessness on the base path lifted the rest of the team. They hit better because the pitchers were rattled and infielders were distracted.

Memorabilia

- Buddy Johnson record, "Did You See Jackie Robinson Hit That Ball?"

- Collectible cards

- Cover of Time magazine

- Jackie Robinson comic book

TRAIL BLAZERS
JANE GOODALL
A LIFE WITH CHIMPS
Every individual matters.
ANITA GANERI

Primate, Monkey, or Ape?

There are more than three hundred species of primates. They all share many features, including large brains compared to the size of their bodies, forward-facing eyes, and flexible limbs and hands for grasping. But, while monkeys and apes (chimps, bonobos, gorillas, orangutans, and gibbons) are both primates, monkeys are not the same as apes. Here's how to tell them apart:

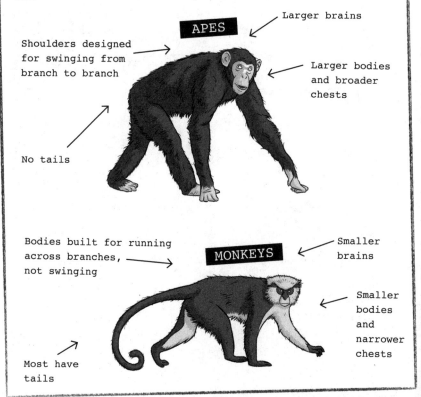

Larger brains

APES

Shoulders designed for swinging from branch to branch

Larger bodies and broader chests

No tails

Bodies built for running across branches, not swinging

MONKEYS

Smaller brains

Smaller bodies and narrower chests

Most have tails